The enjoyment of bicycle touring and an interest in writing and illustrating led THOMAS and CAROL ROSS to write a bicycle column for the *Oakland Tribune*. Highly successful, the column inspired this book.

Active in local affairs, Thomas Ross has also written an urban affairs column for San Francisco newspapers and is author of a novel. Pursuing an interest in art, Carol Ross has taught art and worked in advertising.

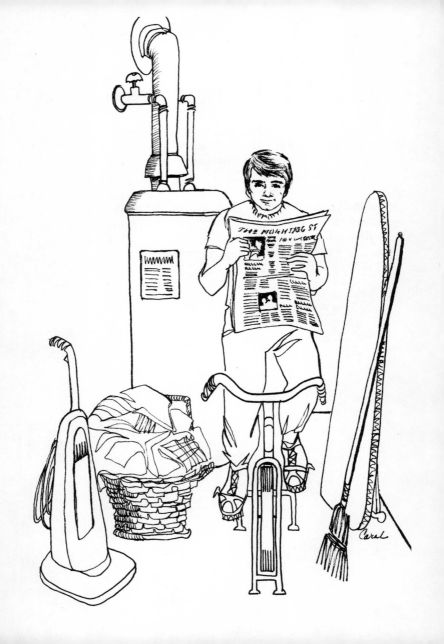

GREAT BIKE TOURS IN NORTHERN CALIFORNIA

BY THOMAS E. ROSS
AND CAROL ROSS

WARD RITCHIE PRESS • LOS ANGELES

This book is dedicated
to
Jonathan, Amy, and Katie.

The material in this book is reviewed and updated
at each printing.

CONTENTS

INTRODUCTION

This book is intended for those who want to extend their bicycling beyond their immediate neighborhood.

We'll gladly drive for an hour or so, especially if we can plan the ride around an outing the entire family can enjoy.

Bicycle tours, however, must be planned. Some bicycle outings can turn into sheer fiascos even for experienced bicyclists.

I can remember riding hopelessly lost along a gravel county road in complete darkness, being chased by dogs and cold, because I relied on an outdated map to which I referred carelessly.

There have also been tours routinely recommended by friends for their scenic qualities, historic values or recreational possibilities that became grim tests of endurance and strength. We assume you want to avoid experiences such as this.

We have taken every ride in this book and many more throughout Northern California. Some rides were eliminated because they were too hilly, others had too much traffic and even wind factors were taken into consideration. A flat ride in the interior valleys against prevailing headwinds can be very tiring.

The rides vary in length from six to seventy-five miles. All of the longer rides have shorter variations. In many cases we have recommended extensions for aggressive riders.

Semantics poses a problem. What seems difficult to one bicyclist may be easy for another. We have taken these rides on journeyman ten-speed bicycles.

We accept hills as part of bicycling and enjoy the scenic variety they bring to a ride. The basic rides we recommend can be handled by Sunday riders. The mileages were taken by a cyclometer and double checked by car. Beginners at touring on a ten-speed bicycle should build their confidence by starting with some of the flat rides. However, even experienced riders walk up grades on occasion.

Northern California offers unique touring possibilities for the bicycle family. The region has open space and a climate ideally suited for year-round bicycle touring.

Our descriptions and illustrations try to capture California's beauty. We hope the reader will find this book interesting as well as helpful.

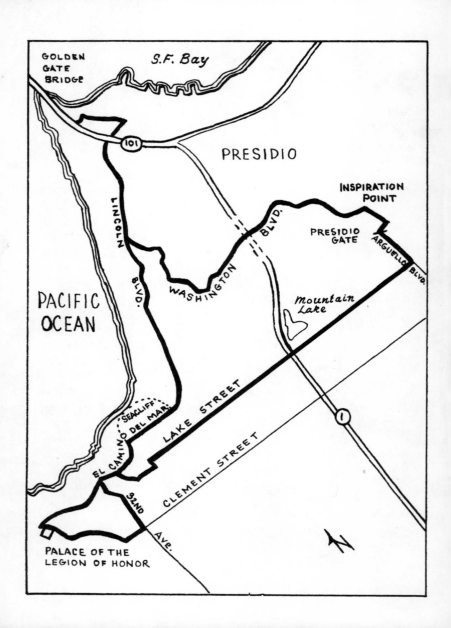

I THE SAN FRANCISCO PRESIDIO

The beauty, romance and mystique that makes San Francisco unique is captured in this picture book ride which symbolically begins and ends at the Golden Gate Bridge. Looking out from the plaza the city's skyline stands at attention, white houses appear in step with the Presidio greenery, waves count cadence against a rock strewn shore and the fog advances slowly through the gate.

The 1,400-acre Presidio has been an Army garrison since 1776. The ride however will avoid the main portion of the base and follow the high grounds to take advantage of the park-like atmosphere. There are some 60,000 trees in the Presidio, mostly eucalyptus, cypress and pine, planted in the 1880's when the post was largely a sand dune.

Turn right as you leave the Bridge plaza on Lincoln Avenue. This is a portion of San Francisco's 49-mile scenic drive. You will cross under the Bridge approach and climb, for a short quarter mile, past some barracks and enter a heavily wooded area.

You are riding above Lands End, the northernmost tip of the San Francisco Peninsula. The side roads lead to gun emplacements constructed as protection during the Spanish-American War. There is a spectacular view area along Lincoln that overlooks Baker Beach, Point Lobos, Mile Rock lighthouse, the Gate and Marin headlands.

A nice coast follows as Lincoln runs downhill for one mile above Baker Beach and past military housing. The Presidio ends here and Lincoln becomes El Camino Del Mar.

Famed Sea Cliff, a splendid residential area with homes overlooking the Gate and Bridge, is an enjoyable side trip.

The only hill on this ride follows one mile up Camino Del Mar through Lincoln Park Golf Course to the Palace of the Legion of Honor. Camino is a mild grade but few people, especially romanticists, make it to the top without stopping. Halfway up, by Lincoln Park's 17th hole, the Golden Gate Bridge is visible. The Bridge viewed through trees, framed by Lands End and the Marin Hills, is a ride stopper.

The Palace, a glistening white art museum, is surrounded by Lincoln Park's fairways. San Francisco's skyline is visible looking down these fairways from the terrace in front of the Palace.

Follow the Legion of Honor Drive through the Park. There is fairly heavy traffic along Clement and 32nd Avenues. Lake Street, which you pick up a short block after El Camino Del Mar, is a handsome residential street with little traffic.

From 26th Avenue to Arguello, Lake has been designated as an official bicycle route and bicycle lanes have been painted on the street. This is flat, city riding.

Enter the Presidio through the Arguello Gate. Inspiration Point inside the Presidio on Arguello offers a panoramic view of the Bridge and Bay. The Palace of Fine Arts appears behind the Presidio forest.

Washington Boulevard is a lightly travelled scenic route that follows the high ground past the golf course and military housing. As Washington approaches Lincoln there are some spectacular views of Point Lobos and the Pacific.

There is ample parking at the Bridge view area and a short order restaurant is also open daily.

The total loop is nine miles and can be handled comfortably by youngsters. For sheer beauty in an urban setting this ride will rank with any in the United States.

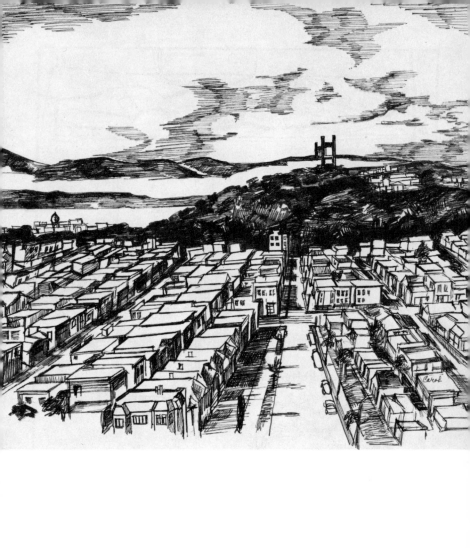

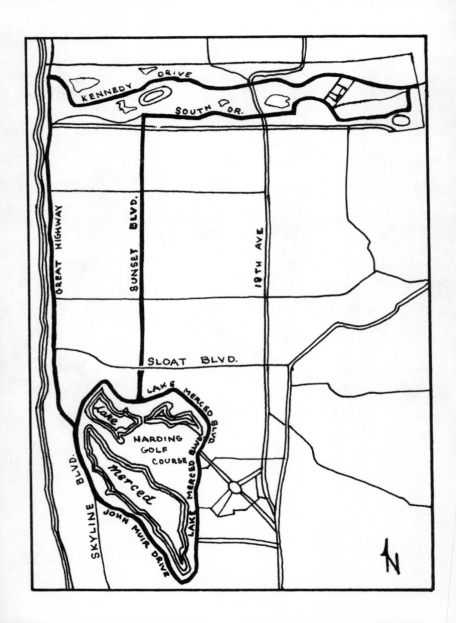

2 WESTERN SAN FRANCISCO

San Francisco's Sunset District is bounded on the North by Golden Gate Park and Lake Merced to the South. Looking West from Mount Sutro, Forest Hill or Mount Davidson, the Sunset District slopes gently to the ocean.

A few years ago barren sand dunes dominated the district's topography. Today, empty lots are few and far between; much of the Sunset is a series of stucco row houses that fill a waffle-like grid running up the slopes.

Four of the City's official bike trails loosely unite the Park, coastline and Lake Merced, making a scenic tour in an urban setting relatively free of traffic. The total loop is a flat twenty miles and can easily be covered in several hours on a ten-speed bike.

Even the weather contributes favorably to this tour. When the dry, hot summers turn inland counties to a sunburnt hue, Golden Gate Park is green and the overcast is invigorating.

This greenery represents a horticultural miracle. The reclamation of sand dunes began before the turn of the century by laboriously nurturing bent grass. Thousands of cypress, pine and gum seedlings were planted which, in turn, provided windbreaks for smaller shrubs and flowers.

Fresh water was found in subterranean streams near the ocean and windmills were constructed to pump this water to a reservoir two miles inland. The windmills are still standing.

The Rhododendron Dell is world renowned and masses of flowers are found blooming throughout the Park in all seasons.

Golden Gate Park is more than an artistic showcase. A tradition of easy access to dells and meadows has been carefully nurtured. In this spirit, bicycling is encouraged as a means of enjoying the park, and a portion of John F. Kennedy Drive is

15

closed to automobiles on Sundays from the Panhandle to the Crossover (19th Avenue) Drive. There are many entrances to the Park but the Panhandle (East) entrance is probably the best starting point, for the ride along Kennedy Drive to the ocean is slightly downhill.

McClaren Lodge, the home of legendary John McClaren, Park Superintendent for 56 years, stands at the Panhandle entrance. Landmarks you will pass enroute to the ocean on Kennedy Drive include the Conservatory with its floral announcement plaque, the Rhododendron Dell, Redwood Grove, Lloyd Lake, Spreckels Lake, and the Dutch Windmill.

The Park is three miles long and one-half mile wide. You are encouraged to explore the many roads that criss-cross between the principal drives. The Polo Field contains a 3/4-mile paved oval that is an excellent track for conditioning and getting acclimated to a new bike.

The Great Highway, along Ocean Beach, contains bicycle lanes from the Park to Sloat Boulevard. This three mile stretch can be quite windy.

Be sure to turn left at Skyline to catch the Lake Merced bike trail. The loop around Lake Merced is a scenic five miles and is the course over which the San Francisco Wheelmen hold their annual Handicap Race.

The bike trail along Sunset is a paved trail located on the Boulevard's west side. Sunset is a very green landscaped route from which there are some nice views of the ocean.

Back in the Park, crank along any of the drives that lead East. Eventually they will lead to either South or John F. Kennedy Drive.

Top the ride with a visit to the famed Japanese Tea Garden located just off the Music Concourse. Bike racks are available in the Concourse parking area. The Garden's 200 Cherry trees generally bloom in early April.

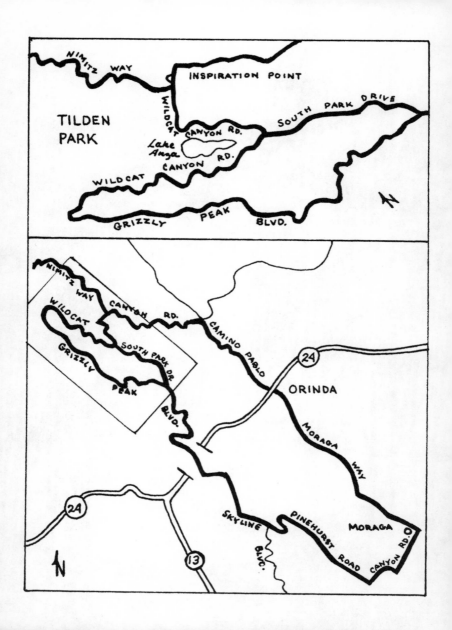

3 TILDEN PARK

Touring in the East Bay combines sweeping views of the Bay and Diablo Range with the quiet seclusion found in wooded canyons and dense forests.

To accommodate bicyclists the East Bay Regional Park District is opening some old roads used as firebreaks for bike trails. One such trail is Nimitz Way in Tilden Park, which is located above Berkeley.

Nimitz Way leads to Wildcat Peak, one of the highest points in the East Bay Hills. The panorama of the Golden Gate, San Francisco and the Bay is spectacular.

Nimitz Way begins at Inspiration Point which overlooks the Diablo Range and San Pablo Reservoir from the eastern rim of Tilden Park. On a clear day visibility extends for several hundred miles.

The round trip from Inspiration Point to Wildcat Canyon Peak is approximately six miles. Nimitz Way is well marked and there is a gate which bars access to cars. Carry your bikes around the gate. The ride is quite easy and the grades are ones that youngsters can handle. This is a good family ride.

There are two picnic tables at Inspiration Point and ample parking; however, if you plan to make a day of this ride begin by the picnic grounds above Lake Anza in the Park.

Make your way down the hill to the intersection of Wildcat Canyon Road and South Park Drive. The botanical gardens and a monument mark this intersection. Turn left on Wildcat Canyon Road and climb for a 1/4 mile to a picturesque view of Lake Anza. The next mile to Inspiration Point has a slight grade and the road winds above this remarkably rugged canyon.

19

On the way-back, intermediate riders might take a loop around the South and North entrances to the Park. The roads are tree-lined and pleasantly cool. There are magnificent views that demand a stop. The exhilarating scent of eucalyptus adds spice to one of the most beautiful parks in Northern California.

Continue on South Park Drive, past the golf course and climb for .7 mile to Grizzly Peak Boulevard. From here the ride is a breeze.

A four mile coast follows through beautiful park and residential areas. The views of the Bay are spectacular. Enter Tilden Park at the north end, through Spruce Gate, and ride on Wildcat Canyon Road for two very pleasant, level miles through beautiful stands of eucalyptus and pine. This loop, including Nimitz Way, is about seventeen miles.

Experienced riders will enjoy the 26.5 mile loop between Tilden and Moraga.

At Inspiration Point continue on Wildcat Canyon Road to the valley floor. This is a very scenic two mile descent with some rather sharp switchbacks.

Camino Pablo is the only stretch where you encounter traffic. Follow Camino, a level road for 2.3 miles, under the freeway, to Moraga Way and turn right again.

Moraga Way is a beautiful residential street lined with a wide variety of rich evergreen, oak and flowering deciduous trees. The road has a well marked paved shoulder. Turn right on Canyon by the shopping center in Moraga.

As its name implies, Canyon is a narrow road leading to the hills. It is a densely vegetated road with one particularly beautiful stand of pine trees that extends for about .4 mile. You climb gradually here and then descend into a magnificent redwood grove.

Canyon runs into Pinehurst and once again you turn right. For the first mile Pinehurst parallels Redwood Regional Park and here you ride through a lush forest of redwoods, oaks, and ferns.

The climb out of the canyon is 1.4 miles and it's a challenge all the way with numerous switchbacks. The view of the Diablo Hills is stunning. At the top turn right on Skyline.

Eucalyptus trees line both sides of Skyline, traffic is very mild, and the views of the Bay for the next nine miles are fantastic. There is a grade for about .7 mile but it is comparatively easy. Cross Claremont and there will be another mild grade on Grizzly Peak Boulevard. From this crest the ride is a joy to Spruce Gate and through the park.

Lake Anza is a spot one really enjoys after a good ride. Here one rests among tall trees with the invigorating scent of Eucalyptus adding to one's sense of accomplishment.

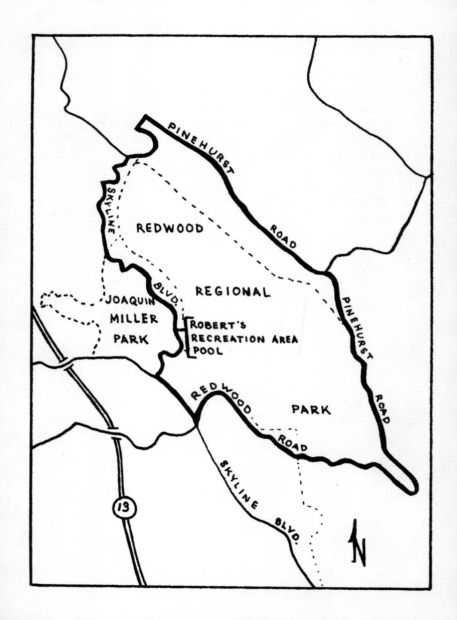

4 SKYLINE BOULEVARD AND REDWOOD REGIONAL PARK LOOP

Bicycling along Skyline Boulevard, which twists and turns for some fifteen spectacular miles above the East Bay leaves one in a very expansive, positive frame of mind. Casual and aggressive riders will enjoy this beautiful region for the touring opportunities are many and quite varied.

At its northern end Skyline is lined with tall, lithesome eucalyptus. Heading south, Skyline bisects Joaquin Miller and Redwood Regional Park which contain a wide variety of evergreens, redwoods, madrone, oak and pine. Outside the parks Skyline becomes a divided boulevard, with a tree studded center strip that is also used as an equestrian trail.

Roberts Recreational Area within Redwood Park has a heated outdoor swimming pool, snack bar and picnic facilities. More rustic picnic areas are found across the road in the Sequoia Ravine area of Joaquin Miller Park which contains dense groves of second growth redwoods. These two areas are a good point of departure for rides in either direction on Skyline Boulevard.

The Sequoia Ravine area has a mile or so of paved road on which bicycles are permitted. Those seeking a leisurely ride should explore this area and head north until Skyline runs into Park and Grizzly Peak Boulevards. There is a very gradual grade coming back which is easy to handle. This loop is approximately six miles.

Aggressive riders will enjoy the 14-mile loop around Redwood Park which contains a number of challenging climbs. On the theory that it is best to end on an easy note, we suggest this loop be taken counterclockwise.

From Roberts or Sequoia Ravine, Skyline drops 1.2 miles to the park entrance. Take a moment to enjoy the view of the Bay from Sequoia Point.

Turn left on Skyline and there will be a series of short descents to the Redwood Canyon Road intersection. Redwood Canyon is scenic road lined with oak, madrone, Monterey pine and redwoods. This stretch is a gradual 2½ mile descent.

At the bottom of the hill turn on Pinehurst (the sign points to Moraga and Orinda). Here you encounter a fairly straight but challenging 1.3 mile uphill that offers nice views of the San Leandro Reservoir and East Bay hills. A 1.4 mile descent follows that will lead through a gorgeous stretch of redwood forest.

Now you must climb back up to Skyline. This is a difficult 1¼ miles with switchbacks; the grade becomes more difficult at the top. Shift into an alpine gear and relax. Walk, if necessary, for the scenery makes this effort worthwhile. The ride from Skyline to Roberts is an easy three miles.

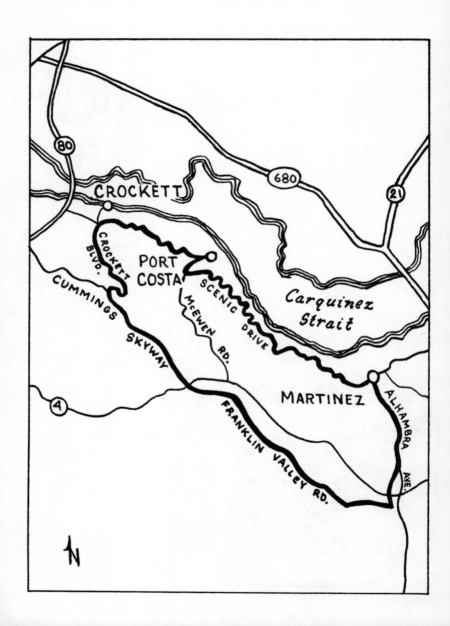

5 PORT COSTA LOOP

At the turn of the century Port Costa was known as the "Grain Capital of the World." Before prohibition, the stock market crash, and competition from inland ports took their toll, Port Costa's business district included eighteen saloons, a dance hall, and seven hotels.

In those days the town catered to barges filled with wheat and grain grown inland. Today, Port Costa is undergoing a renaissance and its guiding spirit, Bill Rich, has a warm spot in his heart for bicyclists.

Rich has converted an old grain warehouse into a three story structure that contains a fabulous Basque restaurant, art shops, and apartments. If you're in the market for Tiffany lamps, metal sculpture, and antiques at bargain prices; remember home-made peanut brittle and old fashioned candy, or collect World War I posters, Port Costa beckons.

Across the street, the Burlington Hotel has been completely renovated. Its rooms are identified by a girl's name; authentic wrought iron beds, marble top dressers, and blanket boxes take you back to Port Costa's more boisterous days.

Plan this ride so that you can top it with a brunch or lunch in Port Costa.

The road between Crockett and Martinez has 107 turns, which explains why it was formerly called Snake Road. Recently it was designated as Carquinez Scenic Drive, a more fitting name. The ride follows the bluff above the Strait, a busy channel used by deep water and pleasure craft. Mount Diablo looms in the horizon.

Traffic here is very mild. The stretch is moderately challenging with a series of short climbs and descents. The climbs are all less than a quarter mile with grades that can be taken sitting down.

Just before Martinez you will ride through a eucalyptus grove and past a cemetery. The route actually skirts the Martinez business district. Follow the yellow divider line and turn on Berrellessa, a one way street, which runs into Alhambra. There is some traffic but the road is wide. After two flat miles, Alhambra runs under Highway 4 and immediately thereafter you turn right on Franklin Valley Road.

This is a pleasant, rural road that veers away from the highway. For five and half miles you will ride through a quiet canyon, past fruit orchards, corrals, and a dairy. Gnarled oaks provide shade and flowering shrubs add a variety of colors. The last mile leads back to the freeway and consists of a very mild grade which may require a lower gear.

McEwan Road leads under the freeway and is the most direct route to Port Costa. This is a narrow country road, that rises very slightly for about a mile. A one mile descent follows on a twisty road lined by eucalyptus trees, on which you'll need your brakes. Taking McEwan cuts approximately 5½ miles off the loop and eliminates a 1¾ mile climb.

Experienced riders will enjoy this challenge.

The Crockett loop requires a ¼ mile climb to the next overpass, followed by another climb up the Cummings Skyway. The grade is mild, straight, and the road has a good shoulder. At the crest you are rewarded by a panoramic view of the Strait and coastal hills.

A beautiful two-mile coast follows, a mild descent with few curves. Pomona Street becomes Carquinez Scenic Drive outside Crockett. You will climb a half mile in two stages, ride above the Strait for a mile, and then downhill to Port Costa. The Crockett loop is 19½ miles.

28

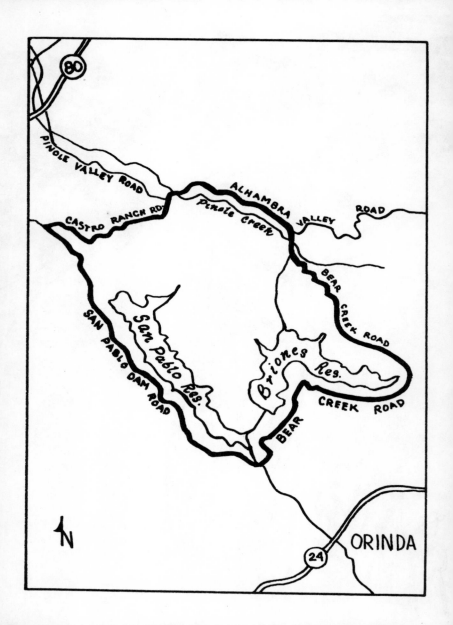

6 SAN PABLO RESERVOIR LOOP

The 19 mile loop around San Pablo Reservoir skirts Briones Regional Park and takes you through quiet grazing land, pleasant valleys and above the scenic East Bay watershed.

This route is a favorite of East Bay bicycle clubs and is used by them for weekly summer time trials. Its climbs, descents and level stretches provide a natural route for improving your bicycling technique.

Ten-speed bicycle enthusiasts who enjoy the exercise and break from routine that touring provides, soon learn to accept hills and even look forward to them. Flat rides, especially at longer distances, have a tendency to become monotonous.

Climbing, on the other hand, provides a terrific psychological lift and sense of accomplishment. Once the technique is mastered, climbing on a ten-speed bicycle is less demanding than one might imagine. All journeymen 10-speed bicycles have low enough gear ratios that permit a slow number of revolutions per minute and enable riders to take any hill at slow speeds.

With these bikes, the advice is to shift into the bottom gear, sit back and maintain the easiest, most comfortable pace the bicycle and your body will allow.

Experienced riders, generally with lighter bicycles, will take hills in a more aggressive manner. They will position their hands above the brakes, shift their weight forward and stand, using their entire body for the downward movement of the pedal. Here, too, the secret is to develop a rhythm and pace that are comfortable.

The Bear Creek entrance to Briones Regional Park is a good place to begin this ride. There is ample parking, picnic grounds at Pear Orchard Valley, and for those in the family that prefer more leisurely pursuits there are trails for hiking along Careade and Alexander Creeks. Most important, by starting here, you take the hills at the beginning of the ride when you are fresh.

These hills are all straight and the absence of trees gives the illusion that the grades are steeper and more difficult than they really are. Pick out goals, every hundred yards or so, such as a tree or shrub and take each hill one "crank" at a time.

Bear Creek Road has a good shoulder and very little traffic. The first hill is a half-mile climb to a point overlooking a corner of Briones Reservoir. The view of tree studded hills and calm water is very idyllic.

Bear Creek rolls at this point and four climbs and descents, all less than a quarter of a mile long, follow. By shifting to a high gear and maintaining constant revolutions per minute your downhill momentum will practically carry you half way up the next hill.

Three miles outside of Briones is a one-mile climb and followed shortly by another half-mile hill. This is the longest climb on the ride but the grade is relatively mild. Beginners will be surprised at what they can do, with just a little determination, in their bottom gear. Go as far as you can, put comfort ahead of speed, and remember that sometimes even experienced riders walk up hills.

After this climb, you're rewarded with one of the great descents in the Bay Area. This covers 1½ miles of basically straight, wide road with a good shoulder. The grade is mild and braking is kept to a minimum. The view on the way down provides a beautiful panorama of the East Bay hills.

At the bottom the road narrows and there is a very short, albeit steep, climb to Camino Pablo (San Pablo Dam Road). Turn right here. The next five and a half miles are easy and scenic pedalling above the San Pablo Reservoir. Much of this stretch is a gradual downhill. There is traffic but the road has a good shoulder.

Turn right again on Castro Valley Road. This five-mile stretch is very pleasant, open country, marked by occasional stretches of eucalyptus groves and madrone. Enroute you'll pass neat rank houses and barns; grazing animals give a relaxed feeling to this stretch.

Your next right turn, five miles later, is Alhambra Valley Road and is marked by a historical marker. Beware, the only road sign is for PEREIRA which heads north to Pinole. For the next three miles you ride through a pretty valley of open grazing land. We met more biking youngsters than cars on this road. Alhambra runs into Bear Creek Road and the Park entrance.

An aggressive rider can cover the loop in less than an hour. Depending on your experience and frame of mind, allow several hours, enjoy the views and plan to spend a little time in Briones Park.

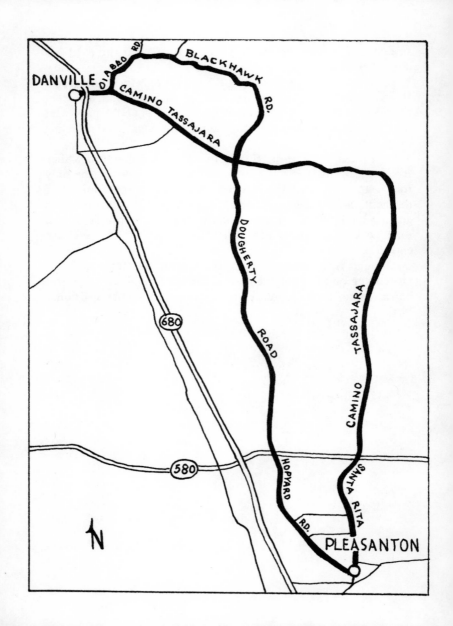

7 DANVILLE—PLEASANTON LOOP

This country ride takes you from Danville to Pleasanton through the Amador Valley in Southern Alameda County. Enroute you will pass neat canals, fruit orchards, and rolling hills spotted with oaks.

Spring is definitely the best time to plan this ride. Following winter rains the hills turn a lush California green, trees are in blossom and the scent of growing wildflowers is everywhere. Farm sounds are with you throughout this trip.

Although you begin in the shadow of towering Mount Diablo the ride is basically flat. What grades exist are very mild and short; the slight dips and rolls add interest to the ride. The countryside is wide open, there is very little traffic, and bicycling along these back roads creates an euphoric feeling.

Danville's most prominent landmark is the Danville Hotel and Restaurant. The Old West is recreated here. In addition to food and drink, the center contains many interesting shops featuring antiques, notions and art work. The Crab Pot offers walkaway crab and shrimp cocktails; the restaurant has a Hand Ore Cart for cook-it-yourself/barbecues.

For those seeking a short ride, there is an easy ten mile loop beginning in Danville that combines inviting open spaces and tree-lined country roads. Follow Diablo Road under Interstate 680 and one mile later bear right on Camino Tassajara. Four miles later turn left on Blackhawk and follow this back to Diablo Road.

To reach Pleasanton simply continue along Camino Tassajara. You'll enjoy this quiet country road.

Pleasanton is a delightful, well planned community, where

amenities such as tree planting and sign control are readily evident.

The town traces its beginning to 1772 when Mexican soldiers, seeking a land route between Monterey and Point Reyes, founded a village named Alisal. In 1867 the village was renamed after General Alfred Pleasonton but a clerical error resulted in its more descriptive spelling.

Two landmarks greet you on entering Pleasanton.

The Cheese Factory, with an outdoor patio, makes an ideal midpoint stop. The Spiliotopoulos family attributes popularity of its cheeses to sampling. A wide variety of factory processed cheeses, imported beers and premium wines are available.

Across the street stands the century old Pleasanton Hotel which served travelers to the gold country in the 1850's. The early California atmosphere is present in the dining room, which overlooks a beautiful garden and bar. The menu is interesting and varied.

Another stop is the Villa Armando Winery, on St. John Street, which is also over 100 years old.

For variety return to Danville via Hopyard, Dougherty and Blackhawk Roads. Because of prevailing northerly winds, the best time to take this ride is in the morning. You might also choose to start this ride in Pleasanton which gives you the benefit of a tail wind on the way back.

The total loop, following the figure eight configuration between Danville and Pleasanton, is 36 miles.

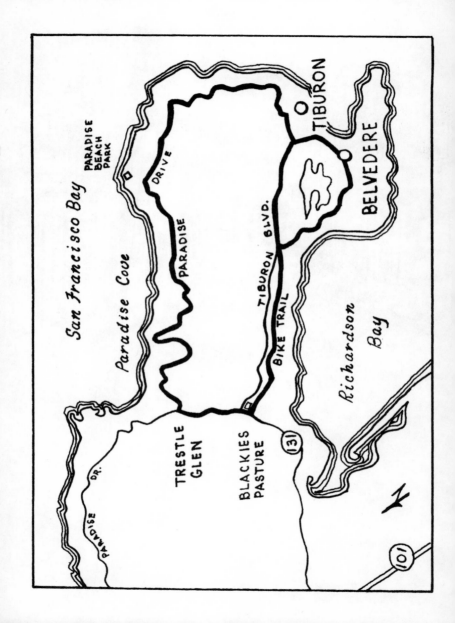

8 TIBURON PENINSULA

At its point the populated Tiburon Peninsula exudes a casual Mediterranean lifestyle that is in marked contrast to the rustic flavor that remains on its backend.

Belvedere's vistas alternate between romantic yacht harbors and the San Francisco skyline. Its hillside houses, secluded by skinny roads, a heavy growth of trees, lagoons, water and fog reflect a lasting love affair with the Bay.

The town of Tiburon and its dockside restaurants has long been a favorite spot to spend a smug few hours enjoying over-sized charbroiled hamburgers, Mai Tais, girl and boy watching, and the San Francisco skyline. In this leisurely climate, browsing through the art shops and galleries on Tiburon's Main Street seems like a staggering effort.

It's little wonder therefore that few people think of the populated Tiburon Peninsula as a likely place to bring their bicycle. Tiburon, however, has some excellent bike paths and it is surprisingly possible, following Paradise Drive, to crank around the Peninsula without encountering any heavy traffic hazards, making this one of the most delightful and scenic rides in Northern California.

Blackies' Pasture, just off Tiburon Boulevard, has ample parking and is a good place to begin. A bike path leads from here to town and is well marked.

The trail crosses Cove Road which leads to Beach. At this point if you decide to explore Belvedere turn right, follow Beach until it winds around a tree and bear left. Beach is narrow and begins with a rather steep half-mile climb (walk this if necessary) but it is probably the easiest road to follow around Belvedere.

39

At Peninsula Point, there is a spectacular view of the Golden Gate and city through a magnificent stand of Pine trees. The view of the bridge is oblique and the white houses of Sea Cliff provide a backdrop for the rust-colored towers.

Beach becomes Belvedere Avenue at this point. Belvedere runs north, through heavy woods, and you look down at Sausalito harbor. This stretch is easy cycling. At the first four way intersection turn right and head downhill on Oak. Keep heading downhill and bear to the right until you reach Beach and Main Street which leads through town.

Paradise Drive is aptly named. After a short climb, just outside of town, the road twists and turns through beautiful, quiet stretches of pine and madrone. To your right is Racoon Strait and Angel Island. The grades, up and down, are very short.

Three miles later, you reach Paradise Beach County Park. This is a grassy area, with picnic tables, overlooking the East Bay hills, the San Pablo Straits and Bay. A pier provides a good place for fishermen to cast a line. The fog generally is gone here by noon.

The next mile and a half follows the shoreline and is very scenic. At the intersection of Trestle Glen, turn left. After a short climb there is a downhill of almost a mile to Tiburon Boulevard and Blackies' Pasture. This loop is about twelve easy miles and can be handled on a three-speed.

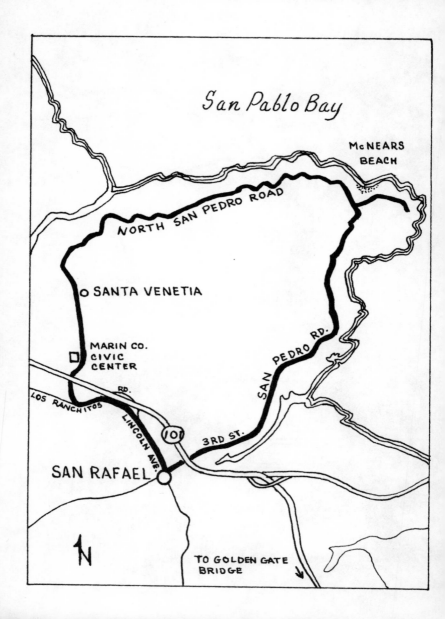

9 SAN PEDRO POINT

Bicycling around San Pedro Point, in Marin County, is a scenic ride, relatively free from traffic, that even a youngster can handle.

For the bicycle family, McNears Beach is the place to begin pedaling. This picturesque park offers a sharp contrast from the rugged country through which you'll ride.

McNears Beach is situated in a little cove on the eastern side of the peninsula. The park is protected from the wind by hills and eucalyptus trees that rim the cove. You can count on good weather here; the customary morning fog is generally gone by noon. There is a large grassy area for sun bathing.

A beautiful ginko tree, with its fan-shaped leaves, and drooping California pepper stand out among walnut and palm trees. Red trumpet vines overhang a protected barbecue hearth and give the park a festive look.

Picnic tables and smaller broilers are scattered over the grounds. A snack bar with indoor tables is also available.

Considering the park also has a swimming pool, wading pool and two tennis courts available on a first come sign-up basis, one might logically ask "Why bicycle?"

This is a stimulating ride that gives one a completely different perspective of the Bay. At several points San Pedro road dips almost to sea level making San Pablo Bay appear endless. The ride swings above the Bay, through countryside, alongside tree studded mountains, and past yacht harbors. There are only three climbs, about a quarter-mile each on this thirteen mile loop.

The first climb is at the McNear Park cutoff. San Pedro Road cuts inland at this point and you'll overlook the Peacock Gap Golf Course and Marin hills from this point. For the next five miles San Pedro Road dips and rolls in easy stages along the Bay. China Camp with Rat Rock, an island close to shore, is very picturesque.

Just outside Santa Venetia, you'll pass Le Chalet Basque, a restaurant with an outside patio. One mile further is the Marin Civic Center, designed by Frank Lloyd Wright. Adults out for exercise might use either of these as a starting point.

There is some traffic at this point but the road has a good shoulder. Follow San Pedro under the freeway to Los Ranchitos and make a sharp left. Los Ranchitos climbs in two stages to Highway 101 where you follow a bicycle path for about 100 yards. This leads to Lincoln Road and into San Rafael.

Turn right on Fifth Street, cross under the freeway to Mission for two short blocks and turn right on Third Street and pick up San Pedro Road again.

You'll pass several yacht harbors and ride past a pleasant residential area. A mile later there is another short climb, an easy grade, with a nice view of San Francisco Bay from the crest. For the next two miles San Pedro runs along the Bay, past Peacock Gap and then cuts inland. A short mile later and you're back at the McNears Beach cutoff.

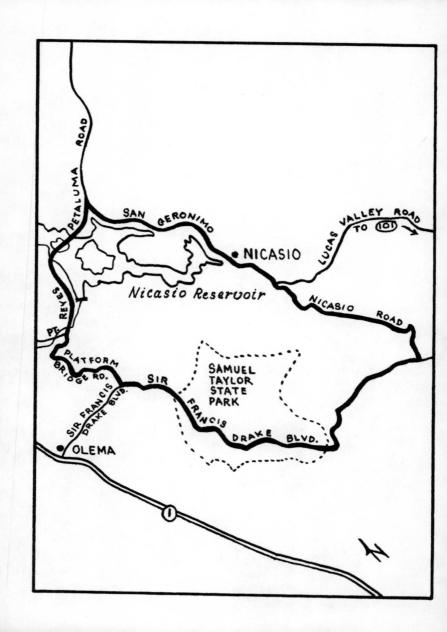

10 SAMUEL P. TAYLOR PARK TO NICASIO

Because of the hills, this is the only loop in central Marin County that can be recommended for the average Sunday rider. It's a very popular ride with Marin cyclists. The landscape varies dramatically on this twenty mile tour that runs through coastal redwood forests, rugged canyons, open pastoral land and past a lazy watershed.

To avoid strong headwinds it's important to take this ride clockwise. Historic Samuel P. Taylor State Park, with ample picnic facilities, is a good place to begin.

The Park marks the location of Marin's first industry, a paper and gunpowder mill constructed in the 1850's. A few years later the region became a popular resort area. The Park's main road is adjacent to Lagunitas Creek, also called "Paper Mill" Creek, and follows the route of the railroad constructed to serve Point Reyes-Tomales Bay. Within the Park there's good cycling through redwood groves and past grassy meadows.

Leave the Park by the Swimming Hole Bridge (walk around the gate) and head north on Sir Francis Boulevard for about a half-mile. Turn at the white barn.

Platform Bridge Road dips and rolls gently for two miles through pleasant country left mostly to cattle. The road generally follows the creek and is nicely tree-lined.

The Point Reyes-Petaluma Road is well-paved, wide, and has a good shoulder. After a short climb you'll reach the watershed and will follow the shoreline to the San Geronimo-Nicasio turn-off.

Enroute to Nicasio you'll pass lonely farm houses whose

47

nearest neighbors are several hills away. An occasional stand of evergreens provides a hint of what's ahead.

Rancho Nicasio is a small village with a charming rural personality. The country church is pure white.

The landscape changes along Nicasio Valley Road from open grassland to heavy forests and lush meadows. You'll enjoy this stretch for the traffic is light and the road has a good shoulder. There is a slight rise to the road and be prepared for a short, rather steep .3-mile climb to a bluff overlooking the San Geronimo Golf Course. The road descends rather quickly for .4-mile, winds past the golf course, and drops again sharply to Sir Francis Drake Boulevard.

For the next two miles you will encounter some traffic but Sir Francis Drake Boulevard has a clearly marked shoulder. The road narrows considerably within the Park and is bounded on both sides by dense second growth redwoods. This makes a detour through the Park practical as well as scenic.

Marin County has a plan to develop a bike path system that includes Sir Francis Drake Boulevard as a major East-West route. Eventually one will be able to ride along a signed or constructed bicycle trail from the Marin Civic Center to Point Reyes National Seashore.

Special campsites, at reduced fees, are set aside within Samuel P. Taylor Park for bikers and backpackers. As in all state parks reservations for these campsites may be made through the computerized "Ticketron" service.

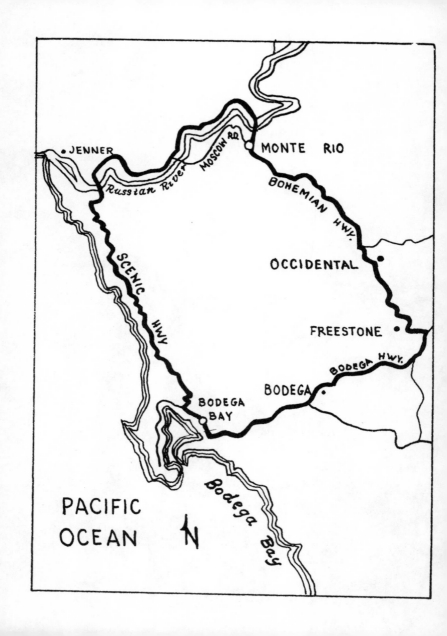

JENNER

Russian River MOSCOW RD.

MONTE RIO

BOHEMIAN HWY.

OCCIDENTAL

SCENIC HWY

FREESTONE

BODEGA HWY.

BODEGA BAY

BODEGA

PACIFIC OCEAN

Bodega Bay

N

II RUSSIAN RIVER TO BODEGA BAY

An emerald surf rinsing coastal rocks, barnacled coves, lonely beaches, salty houses, a high fog, fishing tugs at rest in lazy harbors, pink and purple ground cover, make up the Sonoma Coast.

A few miles inland coastal redwoods compete for sunlight as they have for centuries, at the expense of moss-backed madrone, fir and laurel.

This loop will cover thirty-nine miles but it is basically a level ride that has only one grade, about three-fourths of a mile, which you can walk if necessary.

Start in the sunshine at Monte Rio along the Russian River. There is a six-mile loop between Monte Rio and Duncan Mills, along the Russian River, for those seeking a shorter ride.

Moscow Road, along the south bank, takes you through two miles of heavy redwood forest and then along a meadow beside the river. Duncan Mills is a campground that has a restored railroad station, inn, and store. A bridge crosses the river here; you can return to Monte Rio by taking Highway 116 east along the north bank. There is some traffic but the road is good and there is a shoulder.

Going west, Highway 116 follows the river and is very scenic. After three level miles there is a short quarter of a mile climb to the point above the river and a mile later you come to the Bridge Haven crossing. The town of Jenner at the river's mouth is visible from here.

The bridge marks the beginning of the only real climb on this route. There is a slight grade on the bridge followed by a six-tenths of a mile climb to Shoreline Highway that is somewhat steep. Walk the hill if necessary, for what follows is well worth the effort.

The next nine miles roll and wind along the Sonoma Coast, surely one of the most beautiful stretches of shoreline in the West. There are six public beaches along the way, each with a roadside vista that makes a good resting point.

Outside Bodega Bay, Shoreline Highway becomes Cheney Gulch and cuts inland for five miles through rugged coastal canyons. This stretch is mostly downhill, along a wide road with a good shoulder.

The turn onto Bodega Highway is marked by a sign and a long line of eucalyptus trees. There is a half mile downhill to Bodega, a little town that contains an antique shop, cafe, and general store.

You ride through open grazing land now along a flat road with a good shoulder. Five very pleasant, easy miles later and you pass through Freestone, which contains another cluster of antique shops.

Bohemian Highway to Monte Rio has a bumpy surface at first but is sheer joy as it twists and turns through dense redwood forest. Outside Occidental there is a seven-tenths of a mile grade which you'll take sitting down. The stretch between Occidental and Monte Rio is an exhilarating downhill through the Redwoods, a delightful way to end this beautiful ride.

53

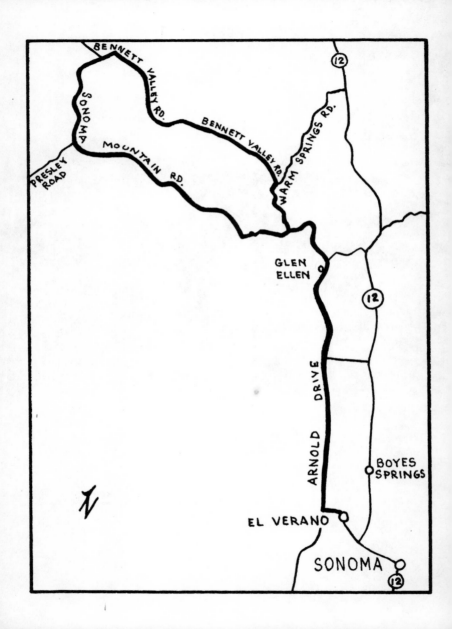

12 SONOMA VALLEY

The Sonoma Valley, also known as "The Valley of the Moon," is one of California's most magnificent. According to Indian legend, the moon rises seven times nightly over this stunningly beautiful valley. The illusion is created because the Valley is narrow and the moon seems to rise separately over each succeeding elevation.

Jack London made his home in the Valley. He wrote: "There are great redwoods in it, deep canyons, streams of water, springs. When I look at it all it makes me ache with the things in my heart I can't find words to say."

Begin your ride in Glen Ellen, located three miles north of Sonoma. London's residence, "Wolf House," is located one mile from here and is now a state park.

A nice short ride takes one from Glen Ellen to Verano. Arnold Drive is a tree-lined road that passes the Glen Ellen Winery and through the Sonoma Valley Hospital grounds. Avoid Highway 12 for it has too much traffic. The side roads, such as Madrone, bisect lush green vineyards and their beauty is framed by the Myacamas Mountains. This is a six- to seven-mile ride.

A more challenging, longer ride climbs to a ridge line along Sonoma Mountain, drops to the Bennett Valley floor and returns to Glen Ellen. This is a hilly route of which the first two miles on Sonoma Mountain Road are especially difficult but the country-side is so stunning that walking these hills is well worth the effort.

Look for the sign pointing to Bennett Valley off Arnold Drive. This is Warm Springs Road, a lightly travelled, tree-lined road that rolls slightly. Turn left at the "Y" onto Sonoma Mountain Road.

For .3 mile you will ride through dense forest with overhanging trees that provide shade. This leads to a meadow, one of many you will pass and a steep climb for .3 mile. Stone Mountain keeps rising in short, steep stages for the next two miles, offering spectacular views of the valley below. A steep half-mile climb, through heavy forest, leads to a crest.

You will emerge from trees, ride past a pastoral meadow and vineyards. A half mile later the road descends sharply through dense redwood forest. Bear to the right at the Pressley Road intersection and continue to Bennett Valley Road. This is open pastoral country.

Bennett Valley has a good shoulder, is lightly travelled, and is very scenic. Its grades are gradual, short and easily handled on a ten speed.

Turn left at the Warm Springs intersection and return to Glen Ellen. This loop is 16.5 miles.

At the end of this ride you'll enjoy a short repose in one of Glen Ellen's historic pubs.

Visit the historic Plaza in Sonoma. Originally a mission, the town was established in 1833 by General Mariano Vallejo who was sent by the Republic of Mexico to guard against expansion of the Russian settlements located in Bodega Bay and Fort Ross.

On June 14, 1846 the California Republic was proclaimed in this Plaza by a group of insurgents and the first Bear Flag raised. Many of the buildings adjacent to the Plaza have been designated as official historical monuments. A day in Sonoma may include visiting these buildings, one of the many wineries in the area, and dinner in a family style restaurant.

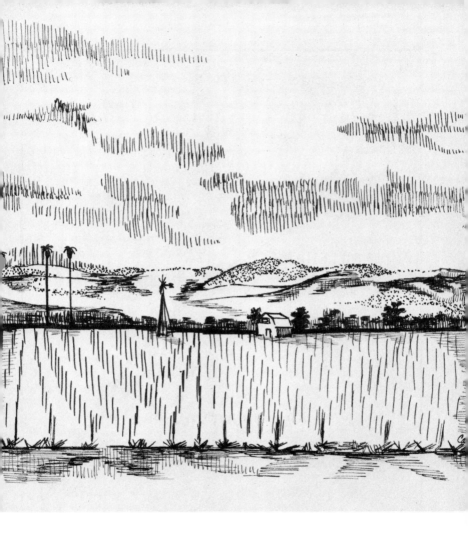

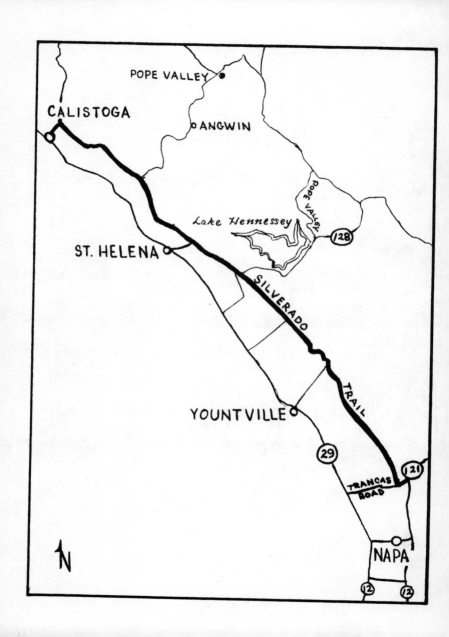

13 THE SILVERADO TRAIL

Tooling along the Silverado Trail one is always conscious of the mountains surrounding the valley. These are tall hills, averaging some 2,000 feet, and they give the valley floor a sense of intimacy.

The hills are heavily forested and provide a beautiful green backdrop for the carefully lined vineyards that dominate the valley floor. The valley seems wider at the southern end and here small hills, perhaps several hundred feet high, add considerable variety to the landscape of the valley floor.

In the 1860's silver dominated the area's economy and the hills surrounding the valley were swarming with prospectors mining silver. The road that runs along the east side of the valley is the romanticized Silverado Trail, named after the squatters immortalized in essays by Robert Louis Stevenson.

Silverado is an analogue of Eldorado, meaning golden utopia, the name given to the Mother Lode area in which gold was discovered. One still captures the utopian beauty of the Napa Valley by cycling along the Silverado Trail. It begins off Trancas Road, outside the town of Napa, and ends some 30 miles later at the junction of Highway 29 outside Calistoga.

This is basically a level ride that a newcomer to a ten-speed bicycle can handle comfortably. Traffic is moderately heavy but the drivers are courteous, and for most of the route there is a wide shoulder.

If you plan to ride only one way on the Trail, there are Northerly headwinds in the afternoon which make riding south from Calistoga somewhat easier.

Route 128 bisects the Silverado Trail approximately midway between Napa and Calistoga. This leads to Lake Hennessey, the Napa Valley watershed. A county-maintained picnic area, with swimming facilities and a snack bar, is located at Conn Dam about a mile East on Route 28. On weekends there is a $2 charge for cars; bicyclists are admitted free.

The Napa Valley is more narrow at its northern end and you feel very close to nature. There are a number of stretches between St. Helena and Calistoga where the Trail takes you through beautiful wooded scenery. On the approach to Calistoga the road rolls slightly but the few grades are very mild and short.

This region offers terrific bicycling tours for aggressive riders who enjoy the challenge of hills. Each year a number of "century" and "enduros" are run which include a portion of the Pope Valley, one of California's most scenic. You reach the Pope Valley by Routes 121, 128 or Deer Park Road. Be prepared to climb; the hills, especially the climb to Anguin, are as challenging as any in Northern California.

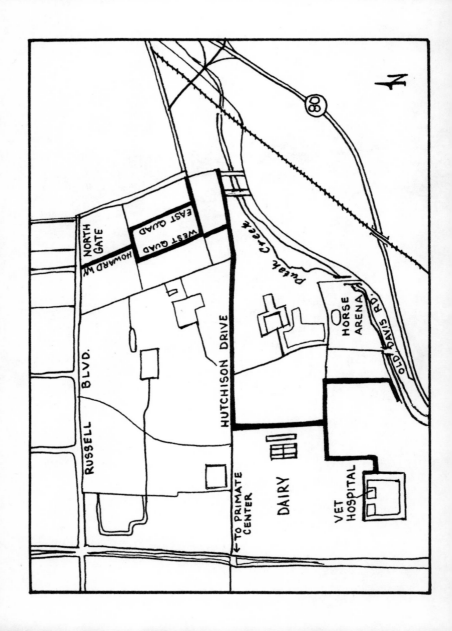

14 U.C. DAVIS

Davis is the most bicycle-conscious community in Northern California and quite possibly the United States. The community has 27,000 residents and over 25,000 bicycles.

City planners consider the bicycle an integral part of the Davis transportation system. Davis was the first community to set aside bicycle lanes on major city streets. Wherever possible, all new street construction will contain bicycle right-of-ways.

Education is Davis' leading industry and bicycles are the major means of transportation for the students and faculty. Indeed, the University of California central campus is closed to motor vehicles and bicycle paths are everywhere.

The flat terrain and absence of autos make U.C. Davis a wonderful outing for younger children. Youngsters with one-speed coaster brake bikes can make it around the campus without difficulty; this "ride" is ideally suited for a baby seat. A School of Veterinary Medicine houses one of the six degree programs offered by UCD, and livestock activities provide many interesting stops for the youngsters.

Leave your car on one of the side streets near the North Gate located on Howard. Detailed maps of the campus are available at the gate.

Howard leads to the Quadrangle which is the heart of the central campus area. UCD began as a University farm and first admitted students in 1908. The oldest buildings on the campus surround the Quad.

Pedal leisurely around the campus, criss-crossing between buildings of interest and head in the general direction of the Dairy Barn. Here youngsters can watch the University herd milked by machine.

The veterinary hospital provides a chance for youngsters to walk among the stalls and chat with some of the interns about the maladies that afflict horses. A short ride along Garrod Drive leads to the Horse Arena where experimental breeds are housed.

Other points of interest to youngsters on the campus include the Primate Center, a pig barn and radiology annex. The Primate Center is located on Hutchison Drive, an easy two miles past Highway 113.

The most scenic bicycle path on the campus is a three-mile stretch that circles Putah Creek. This area is an arboretum that contains many species of trees and shrubs.

A delightful picnic area is situated at the western end of the creek in a grove of oaks. Ducks congregate on a pond at the eastern end of the Arboretum and this, too, is a favorite stop for children.

From the duck pond wind your way through the campus, past the administration building and Law School; cross Shields Avenue to Student Union. The snack area is a good place to recount the day's experiences.

Bike parking lots abound on the campus and stops are very convenient. Make sure you bring a chain and lock, for bicycle thefts, regrettably, are a serious problem.

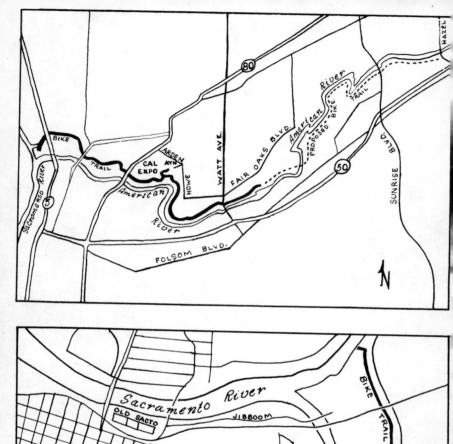

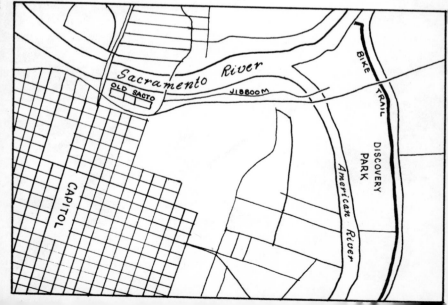

15 THE AMERICAN RIVER BIKEWAY

Cycling along Sacramento's American River Bikeway is a totally enjoyable experience that can be shared by every member in a bicycle family. Combine this experience with a visit to Old Sacramento, the Capitol and Sutter's Fort.

Cottonwood, oak, willow and alders line the trail. Streamside vegetation, including wild grape vines, poppies and lupine grow abundantly.

There are frequent points of access along the trail. The bikeway begins at Discovery Park where the American and Sacramento Rivers join. Discovery Park is primarily a boat launching facility. There is ample parking and a large pleasant lawn on which one can picnic and observe the river traffic.

In its early days Sacramento was continually threatened by floods as the Sacramento and American Rivers swelled from winter run-offs. Following the floods of 1863-4 city leaders decided to elevate the city's grade by physically raising all the streets approximately one story. This was one of the great engineering feats of the 19th century.

Just outside Discovery Park the bikeway runs through a depressed "flood plain" from which fill was taken to elevate Sacramento.

Bannon Slough runs alongside the bikeway for the first three miles. This was also constructed in an attempt to control floods. Because of the heavy vegetation along both its banks, many people mistake the slough for the river.

The bikeway first picks up the river at Cal Expo and follows it closely for the next eight miles. There are prime picnic sites beside the bikeway that overlook the river.

Cycling along the trail one shares the river's beauty and serenity with enthusiasts on rafts, anglers dropping bait for steelhead, youngsters swimming, equestrians and people simply out for a scenic walk.

Eight miles from Discovery Park, the trail leads under a replica of San Francisco's Golden Gate Park. The California State University—Sacramento Campus is located on both sides of the river. The trail ends twelve miles from Discovery Park at Rio Americano High School.

The plan, however, is to construct a pedestrian crossing at Arden Bar and continue the trail on the South Bank through Goethe Park all the way to Folsom. As one heads upstream the river's bluffs, rock formations and sand bars become pronounced. When the bikeway is completed it will provide a commuter route from North Sacramento to the Capitol.

Old Sacramento is an easy ride from Discovery Park. Cross the Jibboom Street Bridge and continue to where Interstate 5 crosses Second and "J" Streets. Walk your bike down the circular ramp.

This area was Sacramento's embarcadero during the California gold rush. Supplies for the Mother Lode were shipped by riverboat to Sacramento and inland by rail. The first intercontinental railroad was planned here and Old Sacramento was also the terminus for the Pony Express which originated in St. Joseph, Missouri. Old Sacramento's historic buildings are being restored and the area redeveloped into a colorful commercial complex. A major portion of Old Sacramento will be developed into a state park containing a railroad museum.

Old Sacramento's alleys and parking lots are considerably below the elevated street level. Between 1865 and 1870 many of these houses were jacked, inch by inch, as Sacramento's streets were raised.

On this ride you will also pass near the youth hostel located on Cal Expo grounds. The hostel provides overnight accommodations at reasonable cost for American Youth Hostel Association (AYH) members.

Many bicycle clubs affiliate with AYH. The AYH sponsors bicycle tours on a local, national and international scale. Membership is open to all regardless of age.

If time permits, visit the hostel.

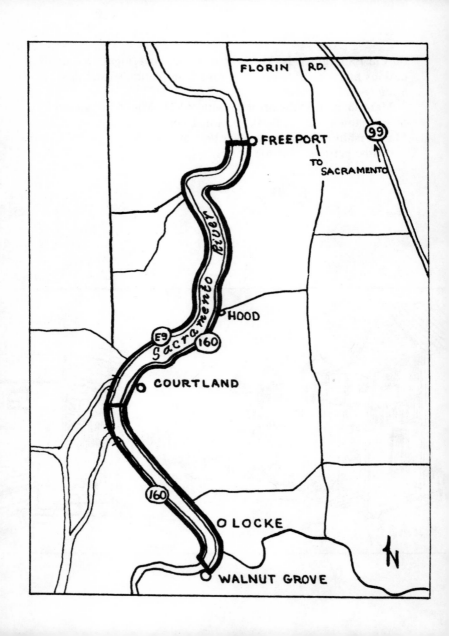

16 FREEPORT-LOCKE-WALNUT GROVE

If touring with a 10-speed bicycle is new to you, the Sacramento Delta is a good place to gain experience.

The stretch between Freeport and Walnut Grove is flat and one can try a longer distance knowing that the riding will be easy. On a sunny day there is likely to be more traffic on the Sacramento River than on the levees.

One feeling that takes hold immediately is the sensation of spaciousness offered by the valley. The road sits on top of the levee which is some 20 feet above the valley floor. On a clear day, the visibility easily extends 50 miles or more.

This part of the Delta region is famous for its pears and much of the farmland beside the road is given to pear orchards. These orchards begin blossoming in February and the blossoms add considerable color to the ride.

The Delta's historic towns are located on the East bank of the Sacramento. Near Hood you will pass some of the stateliest old mansions in the valley.

The houses on the West bank are newer and beautifully landscaped. There are also several likely picnic spots on the West bank.

In the late afternoon, the sun gives a purplish hue to the coastal range and creates interesting reflections in the river.

Make a point of stopping in Locke, a town with a shady past. Historians note the town was first settled in 1912 by Chinese who worked on nearby farms and in packing houses. A fire a few years later, in the Chinese section of neighboring Walnut Grove, fueled Locke's growth.

In its heyday, before World War II, Locke's population numbered 1,500 Chinese who leased their housing from the Locke family who owned the town. Only the older Chinese remain, still leasing the rickety buildings that lean on each other for moral and physical support.

Still standing are the Star Theatre, school, bakery and other retail establishments that served as fronts for brothels and gambling houses.

Stop at "Al the Wop's" for lunch or a refreshment. The walls of this famous pub are covered with graffiti, old posters and pictures of yesteryear. There is also a fully stocked Mom and Pop grocery store and pizzeria in town.

The round trip from Freeport to Walnut Grove is an easy forty miles. On this loop cross the river at Freeport and Walnut Grove. There is another crossing at Courtland, and a loop from Courtland Bridge to Walnut Grove is only 15 miles.

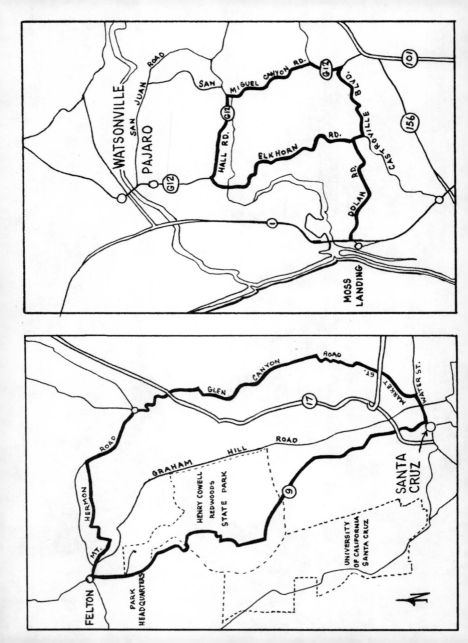

17 WATSONVILLE AND SANTA CRUZ

The San Francisco Peninsula region is dominated by the mountains containing virgin forests of redwood and fir. Its ridge line runs high above the fog which rolls off the ocean and almost daily invades the Bay Area through the coastal passes. For the most part the hills are flanked by ocean and man-made watersheds.

Bicycle touring on the Peninsula proper is recommended only for aggressive, experienced riders that enjoy climbing and can ignore heavy traffic. Many of the Peninsula communities have bicycle routes within city limits but these are token routes. Highway 1, along the ocean, has heavy traffic, especially on weekends.

There are a number of routes in the region which are sanctioned by the Northern California American Bicycle League. These are clearly traced on a standard AAA map.

Most famous of these routes is the La Honda - Pescadero - San Gregorio loop. This ride begins with a difficult two mile climb on Pescadero Road, outside La Honda, followed by several miles of downhill with numerous switchbacks. At Pescadero the route follows Old Stage Road to avoid US 1. Old Stage Road is lightly traveled and has a "camel back" consisting of two consecutive one mile climbs, followed by a downhill with tight switchbacks. The La Honda Road from San Gregorio is easy riding with a wide shoulder and gently rolling terrain. This is a 26 mile loop.

Tunitas Creek Road, leading to Skyline Boulevard, runs through beautiful virgin forest. The climb is one of the more difficult in Northern California and should only be tried by experienced climbers. Low gears are required.

The Peninsula bicycle family has little choice but to travel north, east or south for its rides.

There is a 16 mile loop in the Santa Cruz area that takes in some beautiful redwoods. Henry Cowell Redwood Park is a good rallying point.

Bicyclists are admitted to the Park without charge. A coffee shop is open during the summer season and picnic facilities, overlooking the San Lorenzo River, are available the year round. During the summer there is swimming; steelhead and salmon spawn on the river in the winter.

The Park entrance is one mile below Felton, off Route 9. There is a very pleasant 1/2 mile ride to the gate. Plan to take this ride in the early morning or on weekdays for Route 9 is narrow and a popular scenic drive.

Outside Felton there is a pronounced Y in the road leading to Mt. Herman, a church retreat. The lower road is recommended for it has less traffic, skirts a rather steep grade, and is nicely wooded. There is a somewhat taxing half mile climb into Mt. Herman and the road dips and rises into Scotts Valley. At this point the road is four lanes with a shoulder.

Watch for the left turn onto Glen Canyon Road. After a short 1/4 mile climb, Glen Canyon becomes 3.5 miles of easy down-hill riding into Santa Cruz.

Here you will follow trafficked streets that are ostensibly identified ,as the official city bike route. River Street becomes Route 9.

The high point of this loop is the seven mile stretch from Santa Cruz to Henry Cowell Redwood Park. The road climbs in several easy stages, each approximately one mile long, but the grades are mild and can be handled without too much effort in your lowest gear. At each plateau there are vistas which look down on the wide expanse of quiet forest. In the fall the area's deciduous trees add a warmth to the landscape. Wildflowers bloom freely in the spring.

After returning to the Park, take time to walk the Redwood Loop Trail which leads through famed groves containing trees over 250 high and 50 feet in circumference.

***

Opportunities for bicycle riding in the Monterey Bay Area are limited, especially since the Seventeen Mile Drive has been closed to bicycles! This leaves the flat agricultural country near Watsonville as the most promising for bicycle touring.

Moss Landing, a picturesque harbor on the Bay approximately halfway between Santa Cruz and Monterey, is a favorite destination of bicycle clubs in the area. The round trip from Santa Cruz is approximately sixty miles. This route follows Soquel Drive, Valencia and Day Valley Road, Freedom Boulevard and eventually Pajaro to Elkhorn Road. The Valencia Valley, outside of Aptos, is especially scenic.

A shorter loop for the bicycle family begins on the outskirts of Moss Landing. Start on Dolan Road which bisects the PG&E and Kaiser plants, on US 1.

The ride follows gently rolling roads that intersect fertile farm land and ranches. Clumps of oak, madrone, maple and bay are scattered over the terrain.

Castroville Boulevard has the longest climb on this loop, 1.2 miles, but the grade is quite mild with the only steep part coming .2 mile from the top. This is an easy climb on a ten-speed bike. There is a rather sharp descent directly onto San Miguel Road. Be careful for San Miguel is well traveled.

San Miguel has a good shoulder. There is another mild grade on San Miguel which lasts for about 3/4 mile. An easy descent to Hall follows. Cross here to Elkhorn Road for the longer loop

77

through Pajaro has too much traffic to make it really worth the effort.

Elkhorn Road is a delightful road that climbs a half mile to a ridge line above the slough. Elkhorn is a very lightly traveled country road, lined in stretches with eucalyptus that twists and turns, overlooking the slough.

This is rural country and as most touring bicyclists suspect, farmers raise dogs especially to chase bicycles. The turn of a wheel or cranking pedal sets off a chain reaction in these mutts.

Good sports will concede the cyclist a yard's length and a bark before beginning pursuit; muggers lie in ambush waiting behind a hedge or in a driveway.

How to handle dogs is a matter of considerable conjecture.

A strong rider can generally outdistance a pursuing dog. Stay on your bike if only for the psychological advantage gained.

Carol's theory is that dogs respond to familiar kind words such as "good dog" or "nice dog."

I have found that dogs respect a raised tire pump!

This simply proves that bicycle touring can often be an exercise in communications.

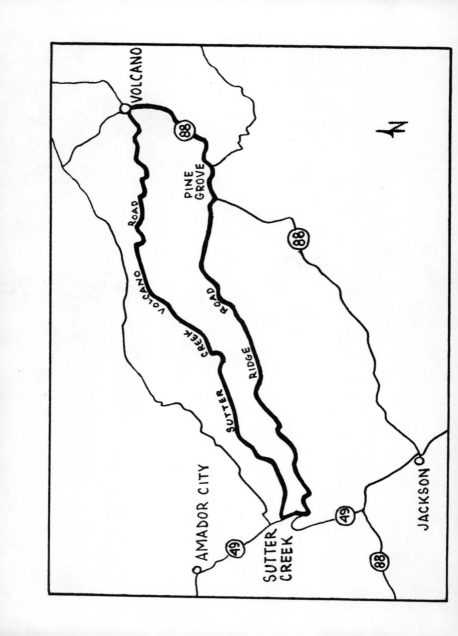

18 SUTTER CREEK TO VOLCANO

The Mother Lode is a bicyclist's paradise. There is very little traffic and the occasional motorist one meets on these back roads is generally considerate.

The sky is honest without traces of smog. Oaks and pines grow leisurely and here the staccato of birds and crickets accentuates the silence. There are grades, some quite challenging, but at the crest of each hill rolling land and sky blend with rugged Sierras.

Autumn enhances these rides with changing colors that create a splendor unique to the West. In the fall bright yellows, warm reds and russets dominate the region.

Every town in the Mother Lode has a celebrated past.

Historians claim that in the 1850's Volcano was California's largest city. During the Civil War, Volcano contained both Union and Confederate sympathizers. The outnumbered Blues smuggled an 800 lb. cannon from San Francisco and "Old Abe" kept the Confederates from taking over Volcano's rich gold fields.

You will enjoy browsing in Volcano and talking with its residents. Visit the historic Saint George Hotel. The ice cream sundaes served at the Jug and Rose Confectionery are surely among the most colorful and creative treats served in the West.

The ride to Volcano begins in Sutter Creek on Highway 49. More famous mines, it is said, were operated within 12 miles of Sutter Creek, than in any other section of the Mother Lode. Taking this loop counterclockwise is definitely easier.

Head south along Highway 49 to Ridge Road. There is a steady one mile grade to Ridge on which you'll work out a few kinks.

You will stay on Ridge for nine pleasant miles that begin in pastoral country, run past a neat vineyard and end in a beautiful forest. Ridge climbs very gradually for several miles and then dips and rolls. Just before you reach Pine Grove there is a spectacular view overlooking Zion Mountain State Forest.

One mile later Ridge runs into California 88. There is a slight grade, on a shoulder, for a half mile into Pine Grove.

The Pine Grove-Volcano Road is well marked. This is a rather hilly road but the steep grades are all downhill.

Chaw'se State Park, two miles along Pine Grove, is a historic meadow that contains a huge rock surface used by the Miwok Indians to grind their corn and berries. There is an Indian exhibit, picnic tables, restrooms, and well spaced campsites.

Volcano is about two miles further, just past and to the right of the Sutter Creek Road Junction.

The return to Sutter Creek is practically all downhill and very easy. This twelve mile ride follows the creek and winds between rather steep hills covered with trees and vegetation. Autumn colors make Sutter Creek Road particularly enjoyable.

The round trip is twenty-seven miles.

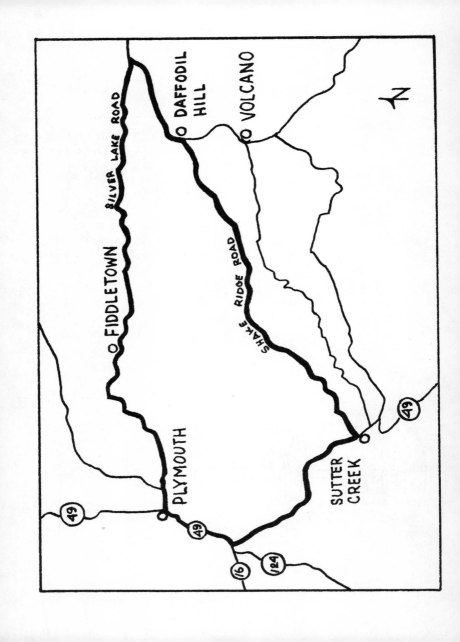

19 DAFFODIL HILL TO FIDDLETOWN

This tour combines a breathtakingly scenic 14 mile ride, practically all downhill, with a timely visit to a Mother Lode landmark.

Take this ride in the spring when the blooming daffodils, tulips and other flowers planted by the McLaughlin family make Daffodil Hill one of the most colorful and unique places to visit in the Sierra foothills. A wide variety of peacocks, roosters, guinea hens and other birds roam freely over the property. Picnic tables are available and on most weekends a snackstand is open nearby.

Some ninety years ago, Arthur McLaughlin bought this land and operated a stopping place for gold country travelers. He supplemented his income by hauling timber used for shoring in the mines. Many of the wagons used for that purpose are still stored on the property.

As mining operations declined and motorized transportation came into vogue, the need for a stopping place diminished. The McLaughlins continued to farm and maintain the land.

Jesse McLaughlin began planting daffodils in volume some twenty years ago for his family's pleasure. Arthur McLaughlin came looking for gold which his son Jesse ultimately found in daffodils. Daffodil Hill's fame is widespread and its beauty is enjoyed by thousands each year thanks to the family's public spirit.

In hilly country, or for longer distances, it is often wise to plan rides with another couple and take two cars. We suggest you leave a car in Plymouth and make this a one way ride from Daffodil Hill.

On leaving Daffodil Hill turn right (east) and follow Shake Ridge Road for two miles. You will begin with a climb of a half mile. At this point you reach a crest that has a sparkling view of the Sierras. The grade is much easier after this. Ride on past orchards, an old farm house and a field that accentuates the mountains.

Turn left on Silver Creek Road and from here the ride is downhill and a sheer joy. There are two quick hills, each about a mile and a half long. The grades are relatively mild and the curves are easy but you'll need brakes. The road follows a ridge and you look over thick pine forests. There are very few cars and one impression that lingers is the inspiring silence of the forest. Be sure to stop and listen.

The approach to Fiddletown is through a picturesque valley. You are still going down but the coasts are interrupted by some interesting level stretches. From Fiddletown to Plymouth the country is pleasant, open grazing land.

Experienced riders will enjoy the challenge provided by the Sutter Creek-Daffodil Hill-Plymouth loop. Take Shake Ridge Road from Sutter Creek to Daffodil Hill. Shake Ridge is a steady series of quarter-mile and half-mile grades. The rise in elevation is approximately 1,500 feet but extends over twelve miles.

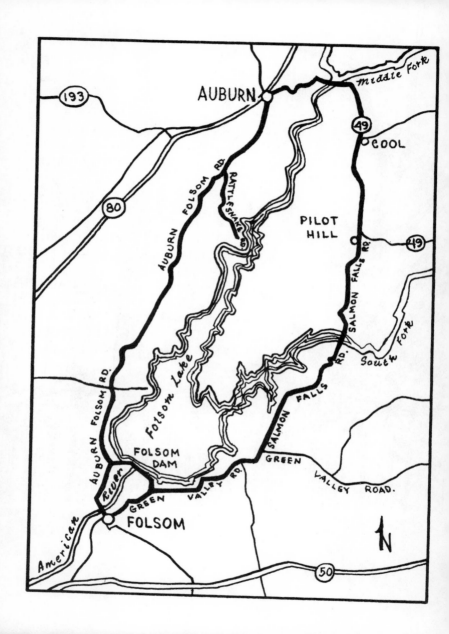

20   LAKE FOLSOM REGION

Bicycling the Folsom Lake region is a year-round delight. In the winter and spring, one rides against the backdrop of the snow-capped Sierra range. Many of the roads are flanked by orchards, trees and shrubbery that blossom brilliantly.

The rush to mine gold in the nearby foothills gave birth in 1852 to the Sacramento Valley Railroad, the first railroad in the west.

This venture, conceived to serve as a transportation link to the Sacramento river boats, fed Negro Bar which grew from a mining camp into the town now know as Folsom.

Pioneer names such as Sutter, Leidesdorff and Judah commemorate Folsom's streets and landmarks; many of the stately homes and churches found in the lower end of town were built in the 1850's.

In 1964, historic Sutter Street was converted into a gaslit mall reminiscent of the Old West.

Its buildings have been renovated and now house antique shops, art galleries, a gaslight theater, and several restaurants, among which is a colorful soda parlor guaranteed to please youngsters.

Historic Folsom is also the gateway to one of Northern California's finest recreation areas, spawned by the American River and Folsom Dam. When the river was harnessed in 1956, an 11,500 acre lake, with some 120 miles of shoreline, was created.

In the summer one can finish a ride with a swim at any of five beaches. Folsom is a warm lake in which the swimming's good until late fall. The area's elevation is high enough to escape the valley smog and fog, yet well below the Sierra snow line.

For an introduction to this area, we suggest you start your ride in old Folsom. Ride along Figueroa Street to see some of the old homes. At Reading, turn left to Natoma and head downhill past St. John's Church and cemetery. The old frame building dates back to the 1850's and is Folsom's oldest church. The tombstones suggest much about life on the California frontier.

Follow Natoma Street to Folsom Boulevard which leads back to town and the Rainbow Bridge approach. The view from the American River is very picturesque.

After crossing the river follow Greenback about a 1/4 mile to Folsom-Auburn Road.

At this point, there is a mild grade that lasts about a mile and a half, leading to Folsom Dam. The approach to the dam is well marked.

The dam appears imposing and you will have to climb another quarter mile but the grade is far easier than it looks. From here on, the ride is mostly level or downhill.

As you cross the dam you will have a panoramic view of Folsom Lake and look down on the American River. There are public beaches at both ends of the dam.

Folsom Dam Road takes you down a mild grade to Green Valley Road which leads past the Folsom Prison peach orchards and back to Folsom.

If you have very young children and tour with baby seats, you might consider beginning this ride at Folsom Park on Natoma Street. The park contains a zoo and miniature railway; there is also a snack bar and rest rooms.

A longer ride follows Auburn-Folsom Road to Rattlesnake Bar, a primitive recreation area near the northern tip of Folsom Lake that is open to the public. This is a 26 mile round trip and a good workout.

Sleek quarter horses, palominos and Appaloosas are visible everywhere in Placer County, grazing quietly in wooded resi-

dential areas or behind orderly white fences that divide the ranches you pass on this ride.

The Log Store at the Horseshoe Bar intersection is a quaint stop. This is a general store with picnic tables and a garden.

The approach to Rattlesnake Bar is a beautiful two mile ride past ranch houses framed by magnificent stands of palm and eucalyptus. Rattlesnake Road slithers quietly along a ridge line that offers marvelous vistas of foothills, meadows, and the lake. In the spring, when the hills are green, the setting is idyllic.

Going around Lake Folsom provides a challenge for strong riders the equal of any in Northern California. Opinions are divided on which way is the best to go. Either way there are two steep climbs by the north and south forks of the American River.

Going counterclockwise there are a number of short but steep climbs on Salmon Falls Road approaching the South Fork. Once over the South Fork bridge, there is a difficult three and a half mile climb to Cool.

The drop to the North Fork is two and a half miles. There are three sharp curves near the top and a straight stretch on which you can let go. The climb up this hill is broken into a two-mile and half-mile section. There are some stretches where the grade is 15%.

The climb into Auburn is a steady 2.2 miles and a challenge all the way.

Except one half-mile climb outside Auburn, the ride from Auburn to Folsom is an easy 17 miles on a slight downhill grade.

In a few years the Auburn Dam will be completed and with it will go half the challenge of riding around Lake Folsom. For strong riders only, this loop is truly one of the great bike rides in Northern California.

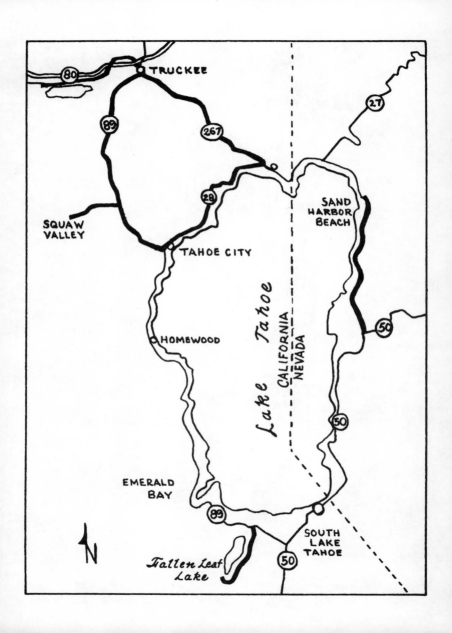

21 LAKE TAHOE REGION

The Lake Tahoe region is so beautiful that it should be included in a book on bicycle touring. Riding around the Lake has become one of the classic rides in California. Keep in mind that the air is thin at higher elevations so take care to acclimate yourself before touring in this area.

One sees many youngsters along the road with tote bags and sleeping bags that take this 72 mile jaunt as an overnighter or stop on a longer tour. D.L. Bliss State Park, Sugar Pine Point, and the beaches at Tahoe City, Sand Harbor and South Lake Tahoe make special provisions for bicyclists.

Most riders agree that the loop around should be taken clockwise to avoid the 1.6 mile grade to Bliss State Park and 2.6 mile Glenbrook climb. The clockwise route has shorter grades to Dollar Point and North Shore, a long gradual climb from Sand Harbor to the Carson Pass intersection, and another climb to Emerald Bay. Climbing to Emerald Bay from Baldwin Beach is considerably easier than the D.L. Bliss hill; the only steep grade is near the very top for perhaps a tenth of a mile.

There are also short climbs when riding clockwise at Rubicon Point, Meeks Bay, Sugar Pine Point and Tahoe Pines.

There are a number of shorter rides within the region that provide pleasant one day outings that can be handled by beginners or less aggressive minded bicyclists.

Sand Harbor is the nicest beach on the Lake. Here youngsters can wade on white sand for some distance in the clear water which, incidentally, is considerably warmer than at some of the other public beaches. Bicycling the nine miles from Sand Harbor to the Carson Pass intersection takes you through State Park and beautiful forests. There is a grade but it is quite mild.

Fallen Leaf Lake is situated at an elevation of 6,375 feet, slightly higher than Lake Tahoe. The approach is essentially level, which makes this a ride that most children could handle even on balloon tires.

Leave your car at Baldwin Beach, which is located about half way between South Shore and Emerald Bay. Baldwin is a very scenic public beach, yet it is rarely crowded. The water is shallow and therefore comfortable early in the season.

The approach to Fallen Leaf Lake is clearly marked on Highway 89.

For the first mile your ride cuts through a proud forest of pine and fir; some 200 feet tall, that grow close to the road.

This leads to an enchanted meadow, a lush green kingdom under the spell of Mount Tallac, a princely peak with a sparkling crown that is worn the year round. Quaking Aspen bring a whispered message of peace in the breeze. A second meadow follows.

Fallen Leaf Lake, born of glaciers and nurtured by Sierra snow, remains clear. For some three miles you will explore its shoreline as the road gently rolls past summer homes that fit in with the lake's rustic splendor.

At the lake's south end there's a lodge and general store. A few hundred yards farther, the Stanford University Alumni Association maintains a summer camp. The road ends here.

On the return you will discover that the road descends ever so slightly and pedaling is a breeze. The round trip is 10 miles.

Top this ride with a stop at the Lake Tahoe Visitor Center adjacent to Baldwin Beach. Run by the Forest Service, the center features a stream profile with an underground viewing chamber through which you observe fish indigenous to the Lake.

The beach, ride and nature area make this an outing that has something to offer every member of your family.

There are some good rides (Ride #25) on the West Shore near Squaw Valley and Truckee.

This is a segment within a thirty-four mile triangle that touches Tahoe City, Truckee and Kings Beach. Each June the Tahoe City Chamber of Commerce sponsors a race out of Tahoe City that is rapidly becoming a highlight of the Northern California racing season. The course includes a steep four mile climb over Lookout Mountain, which probably is the most challenging climb in the region, so the triangle is recommended only for aggressive, experienced riders. The Squaw Valley to Truckee ride, however, can be handled by anyone.

Squaw Valley, the scene of 1960 Winter Olympics, remains one of the picturesque valleys in the Sierra. There is ample parking here. When the snow is gone, horseback riding, tennis, ice skating in the Olympic rink, swimming, and bicycling are in vogue. The approach to Highway 89 is 2.5 miles with a slight uphill coming into the Valley.

Highway 89 is a wide two lane road between Squaw Valley and Truckee that is heavily traveled but offers bicyclists considerable leeway. For much of this 8.5 mile stretch you will ride beside the Truckee River. The pass through the hills is relatively wide, making this a very pleasant, sunny ride. To reach Truckee turn at West River Street.

Truckee's main industry is logging and the town still projects a rugged, old style western image. In recent years some unique moderately priced, little publicized restaurants and shops have opened in Truckee.

On a warm day you might stop at the Stone Cold Inn for one of their "coolers." The Inn is located at the River Street and Brockway Road intersection.

Should you decide to go on, there is a very short, but steep, climb outside Truckee on Brockway Road that leads to wide open Sierra country. For the next five miles you can ride through this meadow against a rugged backdrop of mountain peaks. Brockway Road (Highway 267) is straight, basically flat, and a joy for bicycling.

With the advent of Interstate 80, traffic has diminished on the old Donner Summit road making the ride along the Donner Lake shoreline quite pleasant. The distance between Truckee and Donner Lake is about 3.5 miles. There is a slight crosswind in the afternoons and morning rides are somewhat easier. There is also less traffic early in the morning.

Legislative action promises to save Lake Tahoe's emerald waters from algae but bicyclists would agree that the Lake must be rescued from cars. Highways 89 and 28 need to be widened and paved shoulders provided for bicyclists. The Tahoe region is a beautiful public resource to be enjoyed and shared by all.

22 YOSEMITE

Day breaks first on the rim of the Yosemite canyon and the sun slips, inch by inch, down the sheer 2,000 foot granite walls. Several hundred feet from the Valley floor the sun is slowed by a mass of trees, its warmth cutting through the branches to the ferns and wildflowers that gather around their trunks. All at once the meadows and banks of the Merced River are bathed in sunshine.

Bicycles and cars have equal rights on the Valley floor. The roads are wide and one way. To discourage automobile traffic, the east end of the Valley, from Curry Village to Mirror Lake has been closed to cars.

The Park Service now has Rangers leading bike tours through the Valley on which rock formation, fire ecology and tree succession are explained. The Visitor Center in Yosemite Village also has exhibits that show how the towering cliffs and waterfalls were formed. This is a good place to begin your ride.

Every turn of the head projects a breath-taking sight when touring the Yosemite Valley on a bicycle.

In the spring and early summer six waterfalls send the winter run-off plunging to the Valley floor. The most spectacular is Yosemite Falls which drops 2,425 feet in three stages. Yosemite Falls is the first wonder passed on Northside Drive heading toward the Valley entrance.

Eagle Peak, 3,800 feet above the floor, is the highest point on the North Rim of the Valley. This is one of the Three Brothers, a cluster of peaks named after the sons of Chief Tenya who led the "Yo-hem-ah-ty" or "Oo-soo-mah-ty" tribe.

El Capitan, a sheer granite cliff that rises to a 3,425 foot summit, is probably the most famous formation in the Valley.

For the next five miles you ride through heavy clusters of trees, past meadows and along the Merced River. Northside Drive is one way until the Junction of California 120 and 140 which is a good place to turn.

Highway 41, one mile later, off Southside Drive, leads to Wawona Tunnel and eventually the famed Mariposa grove of giant redwoods. One mile above the floor there is a vista that overlooks the entire Valley. The grade is moderate and the view is so spectacular that this sidetrip should be made.

Southside Drive leads into the Valley past Bridalveil Falls and a series of five massive rocks. Of these, Glacier Point, a smooth grey rock 3,242 feet tall, is most outstanding. At the head of the Valley is Half Dome, a massive rock whose summit stands almost a mile above the Valley floor.

The final loop to Mirror Lake has an easy grade and is closed to cars. Another bike trail leads back to the village.

Fall and Spring are the best seasons to visit Yosemite. Peak visitor loads occur in the summer months. In October the maple, oak and dogwood turn to brilliant fall colors. Spring reaches the Valley in March.

Even in the summer, early mornings are chilly. Warm-up suits and gloves are needed.

There is far more to Yosemite than the Valley. Bicycling opportunities, however, are limited to strong riders because of the extremely long grades.

Both the Tuolumne and Mariposa groves of giant sequoias are within a day's ride.

Yosemite ranks as one of the most beautiful parks in the world. Bicycling in the Park is a rare experience that brings this beauty to one in a very personal way.

INDEX

109

$1.95 EACH—WESTERN TRAVEL BOOKS FROM WARD RITCHIE PRESS

Trips for the Day, Week-end or Longer
ALL BOOKS COMPLETE, MANY WITH PHOTOGRAPHS AND MAPS

QUANTITY		TOTAL
☐	**BACKYARD TREASURE HUNTING**	$ _____
☐	**BAJA CALIFORNIA:** Vanished Missions, Lost Treasures, Strange Stories True and Tall	$ _____
☐	**BICYCLE TOURING IN LOS ANGELES**	$ _____
☐	**EXPLORING BIG SUR, CARMEL AND MONTEREY**	$ _____
☐	**EXPLORING CALIFORNIA BYWAYS, #1** From Kings Canyon to the Mexican Border	$ _____
☐	**EXPLORING CALIFORNIA BYWAYS, #2** In and Around Los Angeles	$ _____
☐	**EXPLORING CALIFORNIA BYWAYS, #3** Desert Country	$ _____
☐	**EXPLORING CALIFORNIA BYWAYS, #4** Mountain Country	$ _____
☐	**EXPLORING CALIFORNIA BYWAYS, #5** Historic Sites of California	$ _____
☐	**EXPLORING CALIFORNIA BYWAYS, #6** Owens Valley	$ _____
☐	**EXPLORING CALIFORNIA BYWAYS, #7** An Historical Sketchbook	$ _____
☐	**EXPLORING CALIFORNIA FOLKLORE**	$ _____
☐	**EXPLORING THE SANTA BARBARA COUNTRY**	$ _____
☐	**EXPLORING SMALL TOWNS, No. 1**	$ _____
☐	**GREAT BIKE TOURS IN NORTHERN CALIFORNIA**	$ _____
☐	**GUIDEBOOK TO THE DELTA COUNTRY OF CENTRAL CALIFORNIA**	$ _____
☐	**GUIDEBOOK TO THE COLORADO DESERT OF CALIFORNIA**	$ _____
☐	**GUIDEBOOK TO THE FEATHER RIVER COUNTRY**	$ _____
☐	**GUIDEBOOK TO THE LAKE TAHOE COUNTRY, VOL. I.** Echo Summit, Squaw Valley and the California Shore	$ _____
☐	**GUIDEBOOK TO THE LAKE TAHOE COUNTRY, VOL. II.** Alpine County, Donner-Truckee, and the Nevada Shore	$ _____
☐	**GUIDEBOOK TO LAS VEGAS**	$ _____
☐	**GUIDEBOOK TO THE MOJAVE DESERT OF CALIFORNIA,** Including Death Valley, Joshua Tree National Monument, and the Antelope Valley	$ _____

[SEE MORE BOOKS AND ORDER FORM ON OTHER SIDE]

☐	**GUIDEBOOK TO THE MOUNTAINS OF SAN DIEGO AND ORANGE COUNTIES**	$ _____
☐	**GUIDEBOOK TO THE NORTHERN CALIFORNIA COAST, VOL. I.** Highway 1	$ _____
☐	**GUIDEBOOK TO THE NORTHERN CALIFORNIA COAST, VOL. II.** Humboldt and Del Norte Counties	$ _____
☐	**GUIDEBOOK TO PUGET SOUND**	$ _____
☐	**GUIDEBOOK TO RURAL CALIFORNIA**	$ _____
☐	**GUIDEBOOK TO THE SAN BERNARDINO MOUNTAINS OF CALIFORNIA,** Including Lake Arrowhead and Big Bear	$ _____
☐	**GUIDEBOOK TO THE SAN GABRIEL MOUNTAINS OF CALIFORNIA**	$ _____
☐	**GUIDEBOOK TO THE SAN JACINTO MOUNTAINS OF CALIFORNIA**	$ _____
☐	**GUIDEBOOK TO THE SOUTHERN CALIFORNIA SALTWATER FISHING**	$ _____
☐	**GUIDEBOOK TO THE SOUTHERN SIERRA NEVADA,** Including Sequoia National Forest	$ _____
☐	**GUIDEBOOK TO VANCOUVER ISLAND**	$ _____
☐	**NATURE AND THE CAMPER.** A Guide to Safety and Enjoyment for Campers and Hikers in the West.	$ _____
☐	**TREES OF THE WEST:** Identified at a Glance.	$ _____
☐	**WHERE TO TAKE YOUR CHILDREN IN NEVADA**	$ _____
☐	**WHERE TO TAKE YOUR CHILDREN IN NORTHERN CALIFORNIA**	$ _____
☐	**WHERE TO TAKE YOUR CHILDREN IN SOUTHERN CALIFORNIA**	$ _____
☐	**WHERE TO TAKE YOUR GUESTS IN SOUTHERN CALIFORNIA**	$ _____
☐	**YOUR LEISURE TIME . . . HOW TO ENJOY IT**	$ _____

WARD RITCHIE PRESS
3044 Riverside Drive, Los Angeles, Calif. 90039

Please send me the Western Travel Books I have checked. I am enclosing
$_____, (check or money order). Please include 25¢ per copy to cover
mailing costs. California residents add state sales tax.

Name _____

Address _____

City _____ State ____ _____ Zip Code _____